PURE HARRY

The Wit and Wisdom
of Harry Redknapp

Published by Carlton Books in 2012

Text and design copyright © Carlton Books Limited 2012

A CIP catalogue record for this book is available
from the British Library.

ISBN 978-1-84732-983-7

Printed in China

PURE HARRY

The Wit and Wisdom of Harry Redknapp

Compiled and edited by
Bernie Friend

CARLTON

INTRODUCTION

Spurs boss Harry Redknapp has been slugging away at the coalface of football management for nearly 30 years. In those three decades, the old-school gaffer has become one of the most quoted figures in the game, sending a tidal wave of laughter across press rooms up and down the country with his honest, witty and no-nonsense views.

Starting his long journey at Bournemouth, Redknapp has also held the top jobs at West Ham, Portsmouth and Southampton, polishing raw talent and fusing it together with experience to create teams of entertainers.

In this collection of quotes and quips from a master of his art – plus a host of glowing tributes from leading football figures – Redknapp voices his thoughts on everything from the invasion of foreign footballers and coaches into the English game, the dietary demands and drinking habits of players, locking horns with the Champions League heavyweights, and, of course, the goalscoring prowess of his faithful wife Sandra.

66 Even when we had Moore, Hurst and Peters, West Ham's average finish was about 17th. Which just shows how crap the other eight of us were. 99

Harry Redknapp *recalls his playing days with the Hammers in the 1960s*

" With the foreigners it's more difficult. Most of them don't even bother with the golf, they don't want to go racing. They don't even drink. **"**

Harry Redknapp *on getting the most out of overseas signings*

" You will never get a better chance to win a match than that. My missus could have scored that one. **"**

Harry Redknapp *criticises Spurs' Darren Bent for heading a sitter wide, in January 2009*

66 Unfortunately, I never had the pleasure of meeting Sandra. **99**

In 2009, Sunderland's **Darren Bent** *recalls Spurs boss Harry Redknapp claiming his wife could have scored a chance he missed*

66 You will never get the sack for having an untidy desk. You only get the sack if you lose games and buy bad players. **99**

Harry Redknapp *offers his wisdom on keeping his job*

66 He took a knock on his ankle, but we played him some Bob Marley reggae music and he was fine. **99**

Harry Redknapp *has his own magic sponge for Southampton's Trinidad hitman Kenwyne Jones, in 2004*

" 'Scummer', 'Judas' and
'Rot in Hell' **"**

Messages for **Harry Redknapp** *on Portsmouth
fans' T-shirts after his defection to rivals
Southampton, in November 2004*

“Come home Agent Redknapp, your work is done. **”**

Portsmouth graffiti after Southampton suffered Premier League relegation under Redknapp, in 2005

66 The future for England looks a bit scary to me. No one should kid themselves England are overloaded with fantastic talent coming through. They're not. **99**

Harry Redknapp *on England's dreadful 2010 World Cup campaign in South Africa*

"Van Persie obviously thought, 'Why take the p**s out of poor old Southampton? I'll get sent off and make a game of it.'**"**

Harry Redknapp *on Arsenal being reduced to 10 men against Southampton, February 2005*

"I never walk in after games and complain about a referee, but this guy is scary. **"**

Redknapp *on referee Steve Tanner, in 2008*

66 John Hartson's got more previous than Jack the Ripper. **99**

Harry Redknapp *on the West Ham striker's disciplinary record*

" He don't speak the English too good. **"**

Harry Redknapp *reveals language barriers with West Ham's Ivory Coast frontman Samassi Abou, in 1997*

" The lad [Abou] went home to the Ivory Coast and got a bit of food poisoning. He must have eaten a dodgy missionary or something. **"**

Harry Redknapp *diagnoses West Ham striker Samassi Abou's mystery illness*

66 I sorted out the team formation last night lying in bed with the wife. When your husband's as ugly as me, you'd only want to talk football in bed. 99

Harry Redknapp's *insight into selecting team tactics*

66 I've seen better fights at a wedding. **99**

Harry Redknapp *on a 1990s training ground scrap between West Ham's Alvin Martin and Matthew Rush*

66 Where are we
in relation to Europe?
Not too far from Dover. **99**

Harry Redknapp *on West Ham's
UEFA Cup chances, in 1999*

66 My missus fancies him. Even I don't know whether to play him or f**k him. **99**

Harry Redknapp *on signing pretty boy Portuguese winger Dani, in 1996*

66 I tape over most of them with Corrie or Neighbours. Most of them are crap. They can f***ing make anyone look good. I signed Marco Boogers off a video. He was a good player, but a nutter. They didn't show that on the video. **99**

Harry Redknapp *highlights the dangers of signing players from videos*

66 Andriy Shevchenko didn't pull up any trees. **99**

Harry Redknapp *on the future AC Milan star after a West Ham trial match at Barnet in 1993*

By the look of him he must have headed a lot of balls.

Harry Redknapp *on West Ham United striker Ian Dowie, in 1991*

" Everyone saw him do it, so it's a free-kick. You can't lie on the floor and pull the ball back just because you've got the hump because you didn't get a penalty. **"**

Harry Redknapp *hammers Manchester United's Nani for handling the ball before scoring, in October 2010*

"In the end he'll come up with some excuse as to why he didn't see it – he couldn't see, he let play go on. **"**

Harry Redknapp *criticises Mark Clattenburg after the referee let Nani's controversial goal stand, in October 2010*

66 Abou retaliated, but the fellow went down as if he was dead, and then started rolling around. **99**

West Ham boss **Harry Redknapp**
on the art of 'simulation' in 1997

" The Arsenal fans hate Adebayor, so I am sure that will make the Tottenham fans like him. **"**

Harry Redknapp *welcomes former Arsenal striker Emmanuel Adebayor to White Hart Lane.*

66 I look at Arsenal's bench and they have Davor Suker sitting there. The man's a legend and would score goals by the bucketload whoever he played for. **99**

Harry Redknapp *hails the Croatian, before taking him to West Ham in 2000, where he scored just two goals*

" From a still picture how does anybody know what Di Canio was doing? He might have been signalling to a team-mate about a tactic. He could have been showing that the score was 1-0. **"**

Harry Redknapp *plays down the one-fingered gesture to Aston Villa fans from West Ham's Paolo Di Canio, in 2000*

" Everyone f*****g jumps all over you. When Michael Carrick gave the ball away the other week there was 20,000 people slagging him off. **"**

Harry Redknapp *bemoans the attitude of fans in the modern game at West Ham United*

66 What do you f*****g think
I said to them at half-time?
Go and f*****g sit back and
let them attack us, or summink?
What a f*****g stupid question.
Genius. 99

Harry Redknapp *interviewed after
West Ham threw away a half-time
lead against Arsenal.*

66 David O'Leary has £30m to spend and he wants to give me £10m for Rio Ferdinand. The day we sell Rio and our other young players is the day this club starts to die. **99**

West Ham boss **Harry Redknapp**
in April 2000 – before Ferdinand
joined Leeds for £18m

66 You can't get f**k-all for a million nowadays. **99**

Harry Redknapp *on caravan-dwelling Dutchman Marco Boogers, who got sent off after 15 minutes of his only West Ham start*

" This is a football club that has been put together by I don't know who, and I don't know how. It's a mishmash of players with people playing where they want to play. **"**

Harry Redknapp *on his inherited Spurs team, in 2009*

"What he can achieve is scary. He has everything – he's six feet, can head it, has a great left foot and great touch.**"**

Harry Redknapp *on Spurs winger Gareth Bale, in 2010*

66 It's scary that they cannot find someone who cares and has the money to back the club up. **99**

Harry Redknapp *on Portsmouth's financial woes in 2009*

66 It don't seem 10 minutes ago. That's what's scary. But I must have been doing something right, mustn't I? **99**

Harry Redknapp *looks back on 25 years of football management in 2008*

66 To be fair, when you looked at our run-in, it was almost scary. **99**

Harry Redknapp *on Spurs' fixture list at the end of the 2009–10 season*

> **"** Harry is very similar to Slaven Bilic, but is scarier in the dressing room if we're losing at half-time. **"**

*Midfielder **Luka Modric** on Spurs boss Redknapp in 2009*

66 No, I'm not a wheeler and dealer. F**k off. I'm not a wheeler and f*****g dealer. Don't even say that. I'm a f*****g football manager. 99

Harry Redknapp *blasts Sky Sports' reporter Rob Palmer, in August 2010*

66 The sad part is that the ones who do well want to go, but you cannot move the ones who are useless. **99**

Harry Redknapp *on wheeler dealing*

If I think too much about next season, I will be scared stiff again.

Harry Redknapp *on Portsmouth playing in the Premier League, in 2003*

66 I was unsettled anyway, so it wasn't as if Milan Mandaric's comments unsettled me at all. I never felt settled in all my time there, unfortunately. **99**

Harry Redknapp *plays down his chairman's role in returning to Portsmouth from Southampton, in 2005*

“The whole thing is a lot of old tosh. It is not true. But let them investigate if they want, let them charge us if they want – I don't care. **”**

Harry Redknapp *hits out in 2006 over claims he was tapped up by Portsmouth when he was Southampton boss*

❝ He said he was tired, and that was disappointing from a young lad. He should be raring to go, but I suppose it's a very long trip back. **❞**

Harry Redknapp on Southampton's
Kenwyne Jones returning from
Trinidad and Tobago duty, in 2005

66 He can say exactly what he thinks of the job I've done. It's a million per cent not a problem for me. 99

Harry Redknapp *on talks with his ex-Portsmouth chairman Milan Mandaric*

" He's cocky and arrogant, but show him a goal and he's away, like a wind-up toy. **"**

Harry Redknapp's view
of striker Jermain Defoe

" I've taken the club forward too quickly. Left the stadium behind, left the training ground behind, left everything behind really. **"**

Harry Redknapp *on his achievements at Portsmouth, in 2004*

❝I wake up Thursday to read I am on the brink of losing my job and going down the pan. I thought I had this dream I had just beaten Manchester United and won Manager of the Month. It must have been someone else.**❞**

Harry Redknapp *on rumours his Portsmouth job is under threat, in November 2004*

" I don't know this guy Velimir Zajec and I never will know him. He will never know me. Never. No chance. It won't happen. **"**

Harry Redknapp *on the Croatian director of football, who took over as Portsmouth boss when he resigned, in November 2004*

66 Lomana LuaLua probably doesn't even know what 4-4-2 is, but when we switched to it he stuck to his position out wide and did a great job. **99**

*Portsmouth boss **Harry Redknapp** after a 2-0 win over Manchester United, in 2004*

66 The only threats I've had this week have been from the wife for not doing the washing up. **99**

*Southampton boss **Harry Redknapp** on receiving death threats ahead of his derby return to Portsmouth, in 2005*

66 It's like being on the *Titanic* and seeing there is only one lifeboat left and we are all trying to dive into it. **99**

Harry Redknapp *on trying to keep Southampton in the Premier League, in 2005*

66 I've been stood there all day
with this plastic angel
in my pocket. I believe in fate
and I'm as silly as
a bunch of lights. **99**

Harry Redknapp *gets superstitious in
a bid to keep Southampton up, in 2005*

❝If I said I'd go back now I'd be crucified – that's all I need. **❞**

Harry Redknapp *on the possibility of returning to Portsmouth as boss, in 2005*

" We went to watch a show, Billy Joel. Half of the foreign lads weren't quite sure who Billy Joel was, but I enjoyed it. For the Charlton game, I'll really punish them – I'll take them to see *Mamma Mia*. **"**

Portsmouth chief **Harry Redknapp**
celebrates a 3-1 win over Fulham,
in 2005, in unconventional style

66 I took Kanu on the Tuesday before the first game of the season as I never had any strikers. He said he hadn't kicked a ball since last season and I asked him if he'd been training. He said, 'Yes, I've been running around the park some days,' and I thought, 'Yeah, I bet you have.' **99**

Portsmouth boss **Harry Redknapp** on Nigerian frontman Kanu, in 2006

66 People thought I had fallen out of a tree and bumped my head when I asked Harry back. 99

Portsmouth chairman **Milan Mandaric**
on Redknapp, in 2005

" To be in the top four alongside teams like Chelsea, Manchester United, Liverpool and Arsenal is incredible. **"**

Spurs manager **Harry Redknapp**
has trouble with his sums, in 2010

❝ I don't like these silly phone-in programmes. People come on who don't know what the hell they are talking about and say things like, 'Sack the manager because the team played crap today.' **❞**

Harry Redknapp *defends axed Spurs boss Martin Jol, in October 2007*

" There has not been one problem. Clive does not come in and tell me, 'You should do that.' **"**

Harry Redknapp *on Rugby World Cup-winning coach Sir Clive Woodward's appointment as Southampton's performance director, in 2005*

66 I will now spend a short period of time to rest and recharge my batteries before contemplating my future. **99**

Harry Redknapp, *two weeks before joining Southampton as boss, after quitting rivals Portsmouth, in 2004*

❝I'm thinking one day about buying Bournemouth. I haven't got mega money, but it is a club I could go and have some fun with. **❞**

Harry Redknapp *on buying his old club, in 2004*

"I was looking out there with two minutes to go thinking, 'Don't do this to me again.'**"**

Harry Redknapp *braces himself for another disappointment on the pitch*

66 Yeah, he's got injury problems. He'll have to call on Berbatov, Ronaldo, Carrick and Scholes. Whoever they put in they will be strong. 99

Spurs manager **Harry Redknapp**
finds it hard to sympathise with Sir Alex Ferguson's injury-list, in 2009

66 We beat them easily, it was so comfortable. Two-nil. An easy 2-0 win. It was unbelievable. **99**

Harry Redknapp on beating Man Utd in the FA Cup as Bournemouth boss in 1984

" That last five minutes was like a lifetime to me. I've headed and kicked every ball out there. When I saw the referee put that whistle to his mouth I can't tell you how fantastic that felt for me. It was like winning the pools. **"**

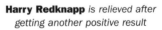

Harry Redknapp *is relieved after getting another positive result*

" Beckham is coming here for the money? Don't make me laugh. He probably has enough money to buy any club in the Premier League, if he wanted. **"**

Harry Redknapp *on trying to bring David Beckham to Spurs in 2011*

" When he picked the ball up, I'd be a liar if I said I thought he would score. I thought he was going to head it. **"**

*Southampton boss **Harry Redknapp** on 6ft 7in Peter Crouch volunteering to take a penalty*

❝ At no time did I use abusive language. **❞**

Southampton boss
Harry Redknapp,
in 2005

66 The referee came over and told me I was spoiling the fourth official's afternoon by jumping up and down all the time. So I said to him, 'I've got news for you, you're spoiling mine,' and that was it. **99**

Harry Redknapp *is sent to the stands at Derby, in 2005, after the Rams scored a retaken penalty*

66 I'm annoyed.
I don't get involved in
transfers in any shape or form.
All I do is find the players. **99**

Harry Redknapp *slams allegations
of making financial gains from agents'
fees at Portsmouth, in 2004*

66 Clive is here to learn. He is not a fool and knows he is not going to walk straight into management with no experience – he wouldn't last five minutes. **99**

Harry Redknapp *on rumours rugby coach Sir Clive Woodward was set to replace him as Southampton chief, in 2005*

" I bought a player and within two weeks he doesn't want to be in England. He doesn't like the way we play and he doesn't like to be tackled in training. **"**

Harry Redknapp *on the gamble of signing foreign players*

66 I've never been in this situation before. My teams might have let a few in at the other end, but they always score plenty. 99

Harry Redknapp *on Southampton's goal drought, in 2005*

66 This is the final straw. You'd have to be a certifiable lunatic to want to work with that lot. **99**

Harry Redknapp *loses patience with his players*

66 At no stage did I ever swear. I just asked the fourth official why the goal was allowed. He said – how you would talk to a six-year-old at school if you were a schoolteacher – to sit down. **99**

Harry Redknapp *comes off second best against a match official*

66 I don't care about Christmas. We are going to train on Christmas Day and we play on Boxing Day. I won't even eat my Christmas dinner – I'm going to be the most miserable person you've ever seen. **99**

*Portsmouth boss **Harry Redknapp** full of festive cheer after a 3-0 defeat at Southampton, in December 2003*

"What are they going to do, shoot me? It's not war you know. **"**

Harry Redknapp *on returning to Portsmouth with Southampton, in 2004*

" If people are stupid enough to shout abuse then they need their heads looking at. **"**

Harry Redknapp *on returning to Portsmouth as Spurs boss, in 2009*

66 Harry was overruled. The club did not want some nutter having a go. **99**

Southampton insist boss **Harry Redknapp** *has an SAS security guard to protect him against Portsmouth, in 2005*

66 I thought Nasri might be captain for them, so they would have to shake hands. Then we could get them in a room before the game and William could bash him up or something. **99**

Harry Redknapp *on making ex-Arsenal defender William Gallas Spurs captain for the North London derby, in 2010*

66 I got the right hump with Gareth when their right-back made a diabolical tackle on him. Then Gareth went for a tackle, bumped in and then walked over and shook hands with him. What are we, the nice guys or something? Let's go out there and compete. **99**

Harry Redknapp *orders Spurs' Gareth Bale to toughen up after beating Arsenal in 2010*

"You tried to hit the goal and you hit me? You've got some f*****g brains ain't ya? No wonder he's in the f*****g reserves.**"**

Harry Redknapp *gets hit by a ball while being interviewed on the training ground at Portsmouth*

❝ If you asked me if I wanted to sell my car and I said 'no', that is the end of it. You don't keep ringing me up. **❞**

*Spurs boss **Harry Redknapp** denies trying to unsettle Sunderland's Kenwyne Jones, in 2009*

❝ I feed foxes, I'm not supposed to, but I love it. The squirrels get a lot – I bought the plastic containers, they chewed the bottom and the nuts fell out, so I had to buy the steel ones. They work better. **❞**

Harry Redknapp *talks nature after taking over at Spurs in 2008*

“ Jamie would meet my dad after the game and take him back to the station with Steve McManaman. Dad said to me, 'I felt bad, as I had a roll for Jamie, but not Steve.' I said, 'A roll? He's getting thirty grand a week.' Every week after he took two rolls. **”**

Harry Redknapp *on his son Jamie, being fed cheese and pickle rolls by his father at Liverpool in the 1990s*

66 You can have all the computers in the world, but your eyes have to be the judge. **99**

*Spurs chief **Harry Redknapp** shakes off suggestions his methods are too old-school, in 2008*

66 No, I haven't sent him the bill.
I just hope he's happy
at his new club. **99**

Harry Redknapp's *reaction to David Bentley
drenching his suit in water after Spurs made
the Champions League in 2010*

66 We've got sports scientists who insist it's important for the lads to eat after games to refuel, even if it's 2am. I used to refuel after games at West Ham until half past three in the morning in a different way. 99

*Spurs boss **Harry Redknapp** raises a glass to sports nutrition, in 2008*

" Kanu? He's about 47. **"**

Harry Redknapp *on the age of Portsmouth's*
FA Cup Final winner Kanu, who claimed
to be 31, in May 2008

“ If you can't pass the ball properly, a bowl of pasta's not going to make that much difference. **”**

Harry Redknapp on Spurs predecessor
Juande Ramos, in 2008

66 The odd indulgence doesn't hurt players from time to time – besides, what can you do? Can you follow a player home to check if his missus is giving him steak and kidney pie for tea instead of pasta? **99**

Harry Redknapp *hits back at England boss Fabio Capello's dietary demands, in 2008*

❝ It's like the *X Factor*. You're either good or you're not. It's not a case of going back, meeting up with the judges for a couple of days, having a chat and saying, 'You should be voting for me really. I'm a sexy bird, I'll get my gear off for you.' **❞**

Harry Redknapp *on England's doomed 2018 World Cup bid, in 2010*

66 It wasn't like Carlos Tevez, who played a few games for West Ham and then wouldn't celebrate for Man City. I had seven years at this club. 99

Harry Redknapp *on refusing to celebrate Spurs' goals against Portsmouth, in 2009*

66 When they got £5m
compensation for me,
they were really happy to
accept the money. In fact,
I think they called a taxi for me. 99

Harry Redknapp *on leaving
Portsmouth for Spurs, in 2008*

" After shooting practice yesterday, I had to drive up the M27 and collect four balls. **"**

Harry Redknapp *assesses the Portsmouth team's striking prowess, in 2006*

66 Modric played well.
Keane, Defoe and Palacios
played well – I don't want to
pick out individuals. **99**

Harry Redknapp *fails to remain
impartial at Spurs, in 2009*

"He came to me and said, 'Futre 10'. I said, 'Eusebio, Pele, Maradona 10 – no, f*****g 16'. We argued. He threw the shirt down, trod on it and left.**"**

Harry Redknapp *talks West Ham shirt numbers with Paulo Futre in 1996*

66 When I heard the news
I thought it was April 1. **99**

Harry Redknapp *reacts to Sven*
Goran Eriksson's surprise arrival
at Notts County, in 2009

66 There is no problem with people having the occasional drink, but if you have to get drunk, you shouldn't be drinking. **99**

Harry Redknapp *appeals for self-control, in 2009*

66 You shouldn't put diesel in a Ferrari. **99**

*Spurs boss **Harry Redknapp** after Ledley King was arrested for drunken behaviour, in May 2009*

❝He is supposed to be our best ref, but if he's the best, I'd hate to see the worst.**❞**

Spurs boss **Harry Redknapp** *after Howard Webb's dubious penalty award helped Man United overturn a two-goal deficit, in 2009*

66 We signed Milko Millman. We thought he was foreign as he came from Jersey. There was another reason behind the deal. At the time you couldn't get tomatoes anywhere – he turned up with a whole box for the manager. **99**

Harry Redknapp *recalls his playing days at Bournemouth in the 1970s*

66 His interpreter is running around the training ground. Sometimes you pass the ball and he chases it. The interpreter is running alongside him and he heads it into the net. **99**

Harry Redknapp *on Russian Spurs striker Roman Pavlyuchenko's lack of English, in 2009*

" He was happy, apart from when I called him John Utaka. Other than that he was fine. **"**

Harry Redknapp *after Jonathan Obika got his first Spurs start, in 2009*

66 I've got a s**t weekend coming up, so has my family and everybody else who comes near me. **99**

*An unhappy **Harry Redknapp***
after Spurs' defeat at Bolton,
in January 2009

66 Palacios is suspended – he likes tackling you see – so I don't know if he'll be any good in our team. **99**

Harry Redknapp *on new Spurs signing Wilson Palacios, in 2009*

❝I've learnt my lesson with the foreigners. I won't be buying any more of them in the near future.**❞**

Harry Redknapp *prior to signing Titi Camara and Rigobert Song for West Ham, in 2000*

66 Nothing at all happened between Hartson and Berkovic. Nothing at all. **99**

West Ham boss **Harry Redknapp** *before realising Sky had filmed John Hartson kicking Eyal Berkovic in the face at training*

" Go on Manny, you play the last 10 minutes son. **"**

Harry Redknapp *sends on ineligible*
West Ham sub Manny Omoyinmi to play against
Aston Villa in the League Cup, in 1999

" We're clearly a top six side, even though the league doesn't lie. **"**

Harry Redknapp *finds West Ham bottom of the table after six games*

66 First of all, I had to find the bloody cabinet. When I did, I opened the doors and out flew two bats, three Japanese soldiers and Lord Lucan. **99**

West Ham boss **Harry Redknapp** on putting the Intertoto cup in the trophy cabinet, in 1999

66 Collymore should have played for England last week. I mean, he is good at beating a Swede. **99**

Harry Redknapp *commenting after England's 0-0 draw with Sweden, in 1999*

66 I was going to pull him off at half-time, but he got a piece of orange like everyone else. **99**

*West Ham gaffer **Harry Redknapp** on Paolo Di Canio after beating Bradford, in 2000*

66 I admire the way he has the ability to turn a situation around, like he has with Tottenham. He's never given me a pep talk, though. **99**

Louise Redknapp *on father-in-law Harry*

66 Some people say, 'You were cheering Portsmouth six months ago, what are you doing now?' I tell them I'm a Harry Redknapp fan. It doesn't matter where he is. That's part of being a family. **99**

Jamie Redknapp *on dad Harry's move to Spurs, in 2008*

" What he might have said, 'F**k off' to him and that was it. What is he supposed to say? 'Go away old chap, stop nutting me.' **"**

Harry Redknapp *on Spurs coach*
Joe Jordan being head-butted by AC Milan's
Gennaro Gattuso, in February 2011

66 I'm happy to go back to London and see Harry, who is a real friend, and congratulate him for all the brilliant work he is doing. **99**

*Real Madrid boss **Jose Mourinho** prepares for Champions League battle with Harry Redknapp's Spurs, in 2011*

❝Give him a team – a leading club side, a national team, even England – and he will be ready for it. He is as good a manager as that. **❞**

Jose Mourinho *touts Harry Redknapp for the England job, in 2011*

❝I just probably looked stupid or something, and they thought. 'Here's one here, he's not Spanish,' and we're looking for a foreigner.**❞**

*Spurs boss **Harry Redknapp**, in 2011, on getting mugged attending the Madrid derby*

❝ I don't get too carried away. I will have a bacon sandwich, a cup of tea and take my dogs out. Life is a rollercoaster and I just try not to get too down or go overboard. **❞**

Spurs boss **Harry Redknapp**
after knocking AC Milan out of the Champions League, in March 2011

❝ It's like a boxer. You might be knocking everyone out, but suddenly you come up against a champion and it's whether or not you can do it against the top people. **❞**

*Spurs boss **Harry Redknapp** on Gareth Bale's destruction of Inter Milan defender Maicon, in November 2010*

" Today was a good day.
Not so much
'Play up, Pompey,'
more a case of
'Party up, Pompey.' **"**

Harry Redknapp *on winning the
FA Cup with Portsmouth, in 2008*

❝ Arry's a legend, ain't he! **❞**

Portsmouth keeper **David James**
on boss Harry Redknapp after
lifting the FA Cup, in 2008

" We don't want that idiot at our football grounds. Make him report to a police station every Saturday for the next 30 years. **"**

*Portsmouth boss **Harry Redknapp** after linesman Phil Sharp is hit by a 50p thrown from the crowd at Villa Park, in 2008*

" He's built like the Incredible Hulk with skill like you've never seen. He's a special talent. **"**

Harry Redknapp *on Cristiano Ronaldo*

66 He used to watch the game like a professor when all the other nutters were jumping up and down, shouting and screaming. Now, he's joined the nutters. In fact, he's one of the key nutters. **99**

*Spurs boss **Harry Redknapp** on the stress getting to Arsenal rival Arsene Wenger, in 2011*

❝ Harry's great strength is his common sense management. He doesn't confuse issues. He is a good judge of a footballer and is straightforward in what he demands of them. **❞**

Manchester United manager
Sir Alex Ferguson *pays tribute to Redknapp, in 2011*

❝ It's a great job, but you pity the poor so and so who has to follow Sir Alex. **❞**

Harry Redknapp *sympathises with Sir Alex Ferguson's eventual successor at Old Trafford, in 2008*

66 A mate said to me after watching Messi destroy a team on his own, that the Argentine looks like the sort of bloke you'd find sitting in a bookies in the afternoon, smoking a fag and betting on horses. **99**

Harry Redknapp *on the deceiving appearance of Barcelona star Lionel Messi, in 2011*

" It seems the Beautiful Game turned ugly this week with that horrible, disgraceful rubbish we witnessed in Madrid. Play-acting, fouling, baiting the referee – cheating, basically. **"**

Harry Redknapp *assesses an ill-tempered El Clásico between Real Madrid and Barcelona, in April 2011*

" The English gave the world football, but while other countries play as well as us, they don't do it the same way. **"**

Harry Redknapp *questions the honesty of foreign footballers, in 2011*

If you ask me, I'll take penalties. We've been practising.

Harry Redknapp *on Spurs' hopes of overturning a 4-0 Champions League deficit against Real Madrid*

66 I drove Kenny to training when he was on trial at West Ham before he joined Liverpool. He scored a goal that was out of this world. Everyone asked Ron Greenwood if we could get him. He said, 'No chance, everybody wants him.' 99

Harry Redknapp *on 'special' Liverpool boss Kenny Dalglish, in 2011*

“ We'd run up the Epping road, cars and lorries flying by, then it was walk and run for two hours. Bobby Moore was always at the back doing it in his own time, while Brian Dear would hitch a lift on a milk float. **”**

Harry Redknapp *recalls pre-season training at West Ham as a player in the 1960s*

66 The captain of England would put a dustbin bag on and poke his arms through the holes so that he would sweat more. **99**

Harry Redknapp *remembers Bobby Moore's weight-busting routine at West Ham, in the 1960s*

66 Barry said, 'I tell you what Redknapp, there'll be two blokes coming down the motorway to shoot your f***ing kneecaps off.' **99**

Harry Redknapp *recalls making enquiries about signing his first player for Bournemouth from Barry Fry's Maidstone in the 1980s*

"When I played with Harry at West Ham, he was just about the last bloke you would have picked out as a future manager. **"**

England World Cup winner **Sir Geoff Hurst** *on Redknapp's managerial credentials, in 2011*

66 We should be able to produce someone who can manage England and let's be honest, they can't do any worse than what they [Sven Goran Eriksson and Fabio Capello] have done. **99**

Harry Redknapp *expresses his views on foreign England managers, in 2010*

" You have got people saying stuff behind you with little kids shouting filth. I didn't bring my kids up to talk like that. **"**

*Portsmouth boss **Harry Redknapp** cops flak off Aston Villa's fans, in December 2007*

66 They have to arrest you to talk to you, for you to be in the police station. I think that's the end of it, it didn't directly concern me. 99

*Portsmouth boss **Harry Redknapp** denies being involved in allegations regarding football corruption, in November 2007*

"Someone has rung up and tried to put £50 on me because they've heard some silly rumour. It's free publicity for William Hill, or whoever it is. **"**

Harry Redknapp *plays down rumours he is quitting Spurs, in October 2009*

66 Harry's doing a fantastic job at Spurs and if he has an opportunity to manage England, I'm sure he'd be an outstanding manager. **99**

Redknapp's nephew, Chelsea star
Frank Lampard, *in 2011*

66 He could be at home now sitting around the pool. I am sure he has a decent enough semi in LA, but he is over here wanting to play football. Most footballers would want to be in LA. **99**

*Spurs boss **Harry Redknapp** on David Beckham's training stint at Spurs, in 2011*

❝ That ball that Van der Vaart hit for Crouchy, David hit about seven of them in training. It was like he had radar and Crouchy kept heading them in the goal. **❞**

Spurs chief **Harry Redknapp** *praises David Beckham's crossing accuracy, in 2011*

66 They're busy cows! I don't like it. I've got no time for it at all. **99**

Harry Redknapp *blasts the WAG culture, in 2009*

" Harry is a very special man, that's why I already feel at home at Spurs. It feels like I'm back on the street. **"**

Spurs' Dutch ace **Rafael van der Vaart** *praises boss Harry Redknapp, in 2010*

"Luka is not for sale. If there has been a bid of £22m that is ridiculous. There are people being sold for £20m who are not fit to lace Luka's boots. **"**

*Spurs boss **Harry Redknapp** on Chelsea attempts to sign Luka Modric, in June 2011*

"Capello is one of the greatest managers of all time. If he cannot make a success of it, it's quite frightening. It's a difficult job and the moment you get it, the papers slaughter you. **"**

Harry Redknapp *on pressures of the England job, in 2011*

> **"**The point is I have a manager who breeds confidence and who is happy to facilitate my odd movements. **"**

Keeper David James, in 2008,
*on **Harry Redknapp** saving*
his career at Portsmouth

" When Rio Ferdinand went in goal, I wasn't too worried. I saw him play in goal when he was a kid and I knew he wasn't very good. **"**

Harry Redknapp on Portsmouth's 1-0
FA Cup win at Man Utd, in March 2008

" When I heard the draw I was on the golf course. I had an eight-iron in one hand and my mobile in the other. When we came out with United, my club went further than the ball. **"**

*Portsmouth chief **Harry Redknapp** on drawing Man Utd in the FA Cup, in 2008*

"We've come here and won against the odds. We've had a couple of beltings and I'm delighted."

Harry Redknapp *on steering West Ham to a shock FA Cup win at Man Utd, in January 2001*

66 Today we didn't capitulate – I think that's the posh word for it. **99**

Harry Redknapp *shows off his vocabulary*

" The most intelligent man I met in football — he's a fox — is Harry Redknapp. **"**

Italian striker **Paolo di Canio** *salutes Redknapp, in 2011*

Bernie Friend is an experienced sports journalist who has covered football for nearly 20 years. He regularly contributes to the *Daily Mirror* and *The People* newspapers and his books include the celebrated *Cycling Back to Happiness*, a two-wheeled travelogue around northern Europe. He lives in Leigh on Sea, Essex.

Sources

The Guardian; The Times; The Sun; The Daily Mail; The Star; The Mirror; The Independent; The Daily Telegraph; Skysports.com; Welcometoportsmouth.co.uk; Whoateallthepies.tv; Soccermotivators.com.